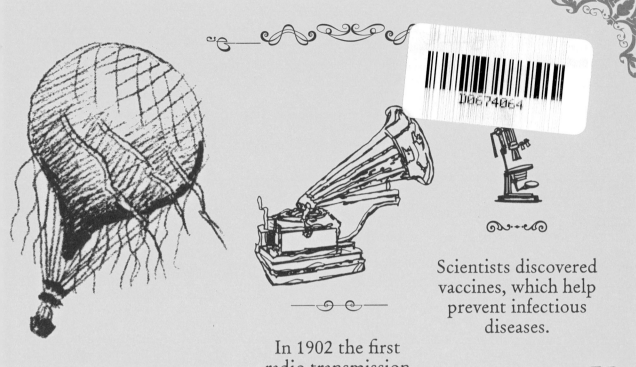

Scientists discovered vaccines, which help prevent infectious diseases.

In 1902 the first radio transmission was broadcast across the Atlantic.

In 1895 the Lumière brothers showed the first film in the history of the cinema.

In the second half of the nineteenth century Japan opened its borders to the rest of the world, and at last people in Europe were free to admire the country's art. Japanese ceramics, prints, kimonos and fans were much admired, and the term 'Japonisme' was coined to describe the works of art and fashion they influenced.

In 1914 the belle époque came to a tragic end with the beginning of the First World War.

The Green Fingers of Monsieur Monet

Giancarlo Ascari
Pia Valentinis

Royal Academy of Arts

Monsieur Monet and his family arrive at their new house in Giverny,
a village in northern France.

Monsieur Monet dreams of a large garden with beds of brilliantly coloured flowers that change with each season.

He employs a team of gardeners and sets them to work.
Later, he gets them to dig a pond.

Monsieur Monet takes great care in designing the inside of his new home. He is inspired by Japanese art and fills the dining room with Japanese prints and decorative objects.

He has a bridge built over the pond so that the scene resembles the famous prints of the Japanese artists Hokusai and Hiroshige.

Monsieur Monet has an eye for fine fabrics.

At Giverny he dresses as a country gentleman,
and has an outfit to suit any weather.

Impressionism

Impressionism takes its name from an 1872 painting by Monet, *Impression, Sunrise*. It was shown in an exhibition organised in Paris by a group of young artists in the former studio of their friend, the fashionable photographer Nadar. The Impressionists were fascinated by changing light effects, and strove to fix on canvas the sensation of a moment with swift, exciting brush strokes.

ALFRED
SISLEY

EDGAR
DEGAS

AUGUSTE
RENOIR

EDOUARD
MANET

CAMILLE
PISSARRO

As well as Monet, such artists as Manet, Pissarro, Renoir, Sisley and Degas were part of the movement. The public initially took no notice, and the critics considered their style of painting coarse, using the dismissive term 'impressionists' to express their disdain. Today, collectors and museums all over the world compete to buy their pictures.

Come rain, snow or shine Monsieur Monet paints in the open air.
When the light changes, so must his canvas, which means he always
takes plenty to work on.

Monsieur Monet is so fascinated by the variations of light and colour that he paints the same subject over and over again at different times of the day and in different seasons of the year.

'I would like to paint the way a bird sings,' he says.
Perhaps he means instinctively, beautifully, frequently
and in the hope that someone can hear his music.

The Garden

When travelling, Monet sent his gardeners letters containing minutely detailed instructions:

'Plant 300 pots of poppies, 60 pots of sweet peas, 60 pots of Argemone (white prickly poppies) and 30 pots of yellow poppies.'

'In March seed the lawn, divide the nasturtiums and take care of the gloxinias and orchids in the hot and cold greenhouses.'

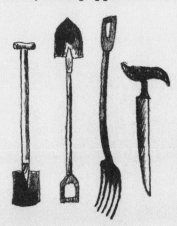

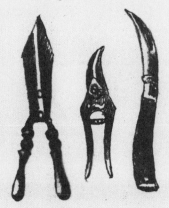

'Water – don't let the roses grow too much, apart from the older and more thorny varieties.'

'In the greenhouse plant the blue sage and the water lilies. Plant dahlias and iris ... If the peonies come, plant them immediately in the ground if the weather permits, but do so in a way that protects the buds from frost and sun.'

'Put iron filings down to make the clematises and rambling roses grow. If the weather is bad make rush mats, but not such thick ones as last time ...'

Monet bought peonies from the English seedsmen Blackmore & Langdon. Later, his sons created a hybrid poppy and named it after their illustrious father.

Monsieur Monet orders bulbs and packets of seeds from gardening magazines. He gathers seeds from wild flowers growing near his garden and scatters them into his flower beds. He wants to be the first to create a hybrid flower with a hue that nobody has seen before.

Friends of Monsieur Monet wouldn't miss the garden
flowering for anything.

Félix Breuil, head gardener at Giverny, is the only person
who knows the plants as well as Monsieur Monet.

The painter spends hours in silence contemplating the reflections the light makes on the pond. One day the water lilies are in bud, the next they bloom.

Monsieur Monet gets up at dawn to look at his flower beds.

He always heads for the water garden to sit in his boat and paint.

The First World War breaks out and Monsieur Monet's gardeners enlist in the French army. The sound of heavy artillery in the distance is a constant reminder of the fighting beyond his garden.

The First World War

When the First World War broke out in July 1914, no one realised the terrible scale of the destruction that was to follow. The 'war to end all wars' pitted Austria-Hungary and Germany against Britain, France and Russia, joined later by America and Italy.

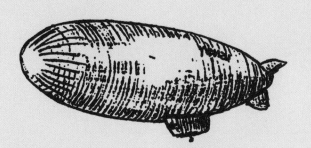

Both the Germans and the Allies built vast systems of trenches that stretched from the North Sea through Belgium and France. This became known as the Western Front. The trenches were sometimes only 50 metres apart and the land between, known as 'no-man's-land', was covered in barbed wire and landmines.

The First World War ended at 11 am on the eleventh day of the eleventh month of 1918. Germany signed an armistice, an agreement for peace, that had been prepared by Britain and France.

Depressed by the fighting, Monsieur Monet closes himself away in his studio. He is ready to realise his ideas on a vast scale and begins painting enormous canvases of his water garden.

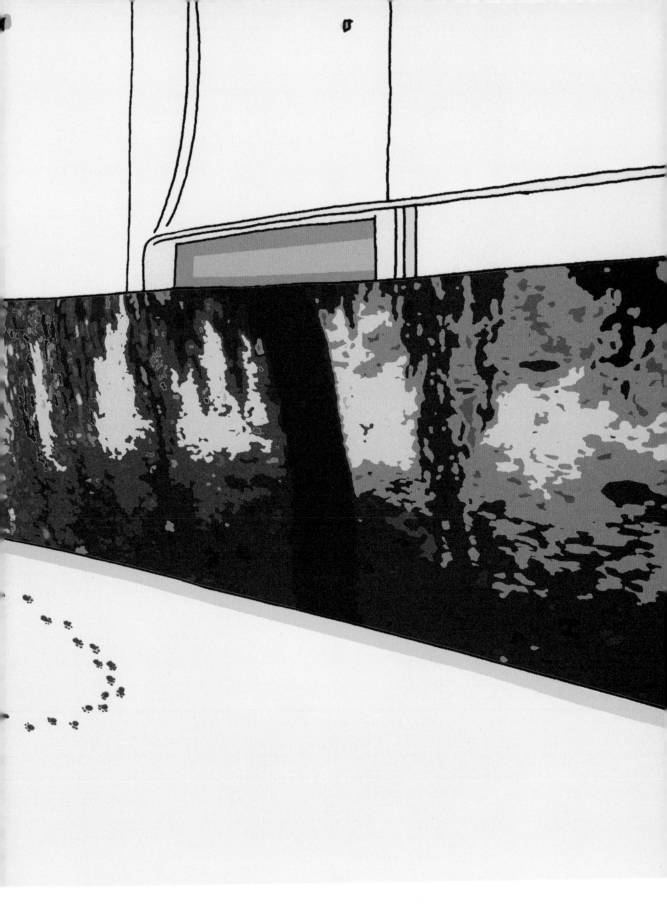

One day these will become one of the art treasures of Paris,
displayed at the Musée de l'Orangerie.

Monsieur Monet continues to work even when his eyesight starts to fail.

His paintings become more abstract as he works increasingly from memory, the water lilies appearing like sparkling jewels floating on a sea of violet and blue.

Monsieur Monet says his garden is his most beautiful masterpiece.
The seeds he has planted have grown into much more than that.

Monet's Life

The French painter Claude Monet (1840–1926) grew up in Le Havre on France's northern coast. He began his career as a caricaturist and was then taught to work with oil paints in the open air by Eugène Boudin. From 1859 he studied in Paris, where he befriended such painters as Auguste Renoir and Alfred Sisley. He was influenced by Edouard Manet and Gustave Courbet and started to show his work in exhibitions with a group of artists who opposed traditional painting. The new style they chose came to be called 'Impressionism'.

Monet travelled between Paris, London and various regions of France, dedicating himself to depicting with swift brush strokes the changes in colours throughout the day and the delicate effects of light on the landscape. In 1883 he moved to a house at Giverny, on the River Seine, north-west of Paris.

In the 1890s Monet began to paint the same places many times over, exploring how a subject can be transformed when it is painted under different light conditions: haystacks, poplar trees and the façade of Rouen Cathedral were the motifs he chose for these series.

From 1908 until his death, Monet's garden at Giverny became his favourite subject, particularly the water garden. Famous writers, among them Stéphane Mallarmé, visited Giverny to admire the changing seasons, as did the sculptor Auguste Rodin and the painter Pierre Bonnard.

A regular visitor was Georges Clemenceau who, while Prime Minister of France, was instrumental in persuading Monet to give his magnificent water-lily canvases to the French Republic in commemoration of the end of the First World War. Twenty-two of these paintings, which Monet had made during the last decade of his life, were unveiled at the Musée de l'Orangerie in Paris in May 1927, and today they continue to remind us of his genius.

Spring

Rose

White foxglove

Lily

Summer

Phlox

Gladiolus

Violet

Autumn

Goldenrod

Dahlia

Aster

Winter

Camellia

Forsythia